Messages From Beyond:

A Parent's Love Never Fades

By: Dr. Daphne Soares

LEGAL DISCLAIMER

The author and publisher shall not be liable for your misuse of the enclosed material. The purpose of this book is to educate and inspire. The author and/or publisher do not guarantee that anyone following these suggestions, or strategies will overcome the challenge. The author and/or publisher shall have neither liability nor responsibility to anyone with respect to any loss or damage caused, or alleged to be caused, directly or indirectly by the information contained in this book.

Printed in Canada and the United States of America

ISBN: 978-1-7380200-5-8

In Loving Memory

July 14, 1940
Oct 01, 2015

Oct 30, 1943
Oct 01, 2015

Frank & Ernestine Pinto

DEDICATION

I dedicate this work to my awesome rockstar parents Frank and E.C. Pinto (Advocate High Court Baluchistan and Sindh, Pakistan). They left no stone unturned in personally raising my brother and I. Their four grandchildren were their greatest treasure. They imparted strong family values and were strict disciplinarians. God allowed them to celebrate their 50-year golden wedding anniversary. Their love was so strong — 24/7 that even death could not separate them. They were both called home together on 1st of October 2015. Dad and Mom, thank you for all you have done for us and our families. You both will always be close to our hearts. Live on, Dad and Mom!

SPECIAL MESSAGE FROM THE AUTHOR - DR. DAPHNE SOARES

Life presents us with countless opportunities and challenges, and how we handle them ultimately shapes our path. Will we allow these moments to build us up or tear us down? Will they bring us closer to others, or push us apart? When I began shifting my mindset to focus on the positive and think creatively, I realized that life doesn't simply happen to us – it happens for us.

No matter how we choose to look at it, life is a precious gift from God. Each person has their own way of measuring its value – some by financial success or material wealth, others by health, relationships, and personal growth. But at its core, life is all about the connections we build, both with ourselves and with those around us.

We often need to pause and ask ourselves, "How well do I truly know, love, and respect myself? Am I seeking validation from others, waiting for their approval, their love, and attention?" The more you nurture yourself, the more you have to give, and when you give from a place of abundance, that love flows freely. Learning to love yourself is the first step to being able to love others deeply. You cannot pour from an empty cup.

In my experience as a business and leadership coach, counselor and NLP Master Practitioner, I have discovered that the relationship you cultivate with yourself is key to growth and fulfillment. No one can truly know you better than you know yourself, and connecting with your inner self is what allows you to flourish.

As women, there are so many expectations placed upon us. Society often implies that we should be seen but not heard. But why? Don't women have voices, dreams, and feelings that deserve to be acknowledged? We are far more than caretakers, homemakers, or mothers – though those roles are important. We are created for greatness, with a divine purpose. In partnership, men and women are equals, both carrying the responsibility of building a home and raising children together.

I learned this firsthand from my parents, whose partnership was a model of shared responsibility and love. I've carried these lessons with me into adulthood, passing them along to my own children, clients, and community. As a working mother and entrepreneur, I understand how overwhelming it can be to balance all the demands of life. That's why it's so crucial to let your family share in the responsibilities, and to make sure you carve out time for yourself. Prioritizing "ME time" to recharge is not selfish – it's an essential act of self-care and love.

Take time to make those around you feel valued. Listen to them and show them that they matter, and you care. Cherish the moments with your loved ones, for time is fleeting, and the memories you create together will last a lifetime and beyond. Don't dwell on past regrets. Grief and loss are a natural part of life, but the true question is, *"Did you make time for those you loved when they were still with you?"* Memories are priceless, and they help us carry on through the pain of loss.

As you read through my book ‘Messages From Beyond: A Parent’s Love Never Fades’, my hope is that you find wisdom and understanding that love beyond life involves embracing the idea that love transcends the physical boundaries of our existence.

FOREWORD

It is with immense pride and a full heart that I write this foreword for my mother, Dr. Daphne Soares, as she shares her journey through loss, healing, and connection in her new book, 'Messages from Beyond: A Parent's Love Never Fades'. This powerful work is dedicated to my grandparents, E.C. Pinto (Advocate High Court Baluchistan and Sindh, Pakistan) and Frank Pinto, whose love, values and influence continue to guide and inspire our family at every step.

My grandmother was a woman of great intellect, strength, and compassion. Her wisdom and leadership were matched by my grandfather, Frank Pinto, whose love for his family created a foundation of support and care. Together, they left a legacy that is beautifully captured in this book—one that speaks to the unbreakable bond between parents and their children, even beyond the physical realm.

As my mother reflects on her own experiences of love, loss, and the enduring connection with her parents, she offers readers a glimpse into the comfort and peace that come from knowing that a parent's love never truly fades. My brother and I have had the privilege of witnessing her strength firsthand, and we are constantly reminded of the love that continues to flow from our grandparents through her.

My uncle, Ashley Pinto, my mothers' brother and family, share in this deep connection, and together, we honour the memories of our grandparents. This book is not just a tribute to their lives but also a guide for anyone seeking to find solace in the enduring presence of their loved ones.

Messages from Beyond is a testament to the eternal nature of love—a love that transcends loss and speaks to the heart of what it means to be part of a family. My mother's words are a gift to all of us, offering hope and reassurance that the love we share with our parents continues to shape our lives, even from beyond.

It is my deepest hope, and my brother's as well, that this book will bring comfort and understanding to those who read it, allowing them to connect with the eternal presence of their loved ones in spirit. My mother's journey is one of grace, and her ability to transform pain into purpose is a message of hope for us all.

With love and gratitude,
Kit Soares

ACKNOWLEGEMENTS:

I want to start by giving thanks to the good Lord for His grace and the countless blessings He has poured into my life. I am forever grateful for His guidance and for the amazing people He has brought my way.

To my parents, E.C. Pinto (Advocate High Court Baluchistan and Sindh) and Frank Pinto who gave me the gift of life and instilled in me unwavering belief — I thank you both from the bottom of my heart. Dad, your sense of discipline and knack for organization have always been traits I admired. Mum, your love for education has encouraged me to chase my dreams and aim for the stars. It has shaped who I am today. I owe so much of who I've become to the example you both set for me.

I also extend my deepest gratitude to my mentors — Tony Robbins, Dean Graziosi, Les Brown, Richmond Dinh, Tony Kaye, Dayton University, ABNLP, and the Anugraha Capuchin Institute of Counseling and Psychotherapy.

Your teachings have left a lasting impact on my journey.

To my husband, Lawrence, the love of my life, I thank you for always believing in me and trusting my abilities. And to our wonderful children, you are my strength and support, and I am grateful for you each day.

To my brother, Ashley and family, who has always been a constant support and guide in my life and has now taken on a fatherly role in our family, I cannot thank you enough for your love and support.

To my dearest friend Jasmine, who has given up her sleeps in assisting me in editing this book and adding the final touches.

Lastly, to my dear home country, Pakistan — thank you for shaping my identity and recognizing my efforts. You have played such an important role in my life.

TABLE OF CONTENTS

Chapter 1:
The Unbreakable Bond

UNDERSTANDING LOVE BEYOND LIFE

Understanding love beyond life involves embracing the idea that love transcends the physical boundaries of our existence. For those who have experienced the profound loss of a parent, this concept can offer a source of comfort and hope. It suggests that the emotional bonds formed during our time together are not severed by death but instead transform into a different, enduring connection. This belief can help you find solace in the knowledge that your loved one continues to exist in a different form, reminding you that the essence of your relationship remains intact.

When we talk about love that never dies, we must acknowledge the depth of the emotional ties that bind us to our parents. Those moments of laughter, guidance, and unconditional support create a tapestry of memories that shape who we are. Even after their physical presence is gone, these cherished memories can serve as a reminder that love is not confined to the here and now. The strength of this love can empower you to navigate your grief, knowing that your parent's spirit lives on in your heart and the lessons they imparted continue to guide your journey.

Spiritual connections offer another layer to understanding love beyond life. Many individuals report feeling their loved ones' presence in moments of quiet reflection or during significant life events. These experiences can manifest as a sense of warmth, a gentle whisper in the wind, or even dreams that feel more vivid than reality. Believing in these spiritual connections can help you maintain a bond with your parent, allowing you to feel their love enveloping you in times of need. This connection serves as a reminder that love is a powerful force that can bridge the gap between the physical and spiritual realms.

In embracing the concept of love beyond life, it is essential to cultivate practices that honor and nurture this relationship. Engaging in rituals, such as lighting a candle in their memory or writing letters to your parent, can create a sacred space for connection. Sharing stories and celebrating their life with family and friends can also help keep their spirit alive. These actions not only honor their memory but also reinforce the belief that your love remains a vibrant thread connecting you to them, even if they are no longer physically present.

Ultimately, understanding love beyond life can transform the way you experience grief. Instead of viewing loss as an end, you can see it as a continuation of your relationship in a new dimension. By allowing this perspective to take root, you can find peace in knowing that your parent's love will always be a part of who you are, guiding you as you move forward. This journey of understanding can illuminate the path through your grief, reminding you that true love never dies, and the bonds we share can withstand the test of time and space.

THE NATURE OF SPIRITUAL CONNECTIONS

Spiritual connections transcend the boundaries of the physical world, offering a profound understanding of love that continues beyond the earthly experience. For those who have lost a parent, the ache of absence can be overwhelming. Yet, within that sorrow lies the potential for a deeper bond, one that exists in the realm of spirit. As we navigate life's challenges, it's essential to recognize that our loved ones remain with us in ways that are often unseen but deeply felt. This connection can bring comfort, guidance, and a sense of peace, reminding us that love truly never dies.

The nature of these spiritual connections is rooted in the belief that love is a powerful force that cannot be extinguished by death. Many individuals report experiencing signs or messages from their departed loved ones, whether through dreams, sudden feelings of warmth, or unexpected memories that flood their minds. These moments serve as gentle reminders that the essence of our parents remains intertwined with our existence. Embracing the idea that our loved ones are still present in spirit can help alleviate feelings of loneliness and despair, allowing us to find solace in the ongoing relationship we share.

Furthermore, spiritual connections can manifest in various forms, often tailored to the unique bond shared between a parent and child. Some individuals find comfort in the natural world, experiencing a sense of their parent's presence in a beautiful sunset, a gentle breeze, or the rustling of leaves. Others may hear familiar songs that evoke cherished memories or notice coincidences that seem too significant to be mere chance. These occurrences can serve as affirmations of love, encouraging us to pay attention to the signs that surround us. By remaining open to these experiences, we can cultivate a sense of connection that nourishes our hearts.

Engaging in practices such as meditation, prayer, or journaling can also enhance our ability to connect with the spirit of our loved ones. These tools create a sacred space for reflection and communication, allowing us to express our feelings and invite our parents' presence into our lives. As we explore these practices, we may discover a wealth of insights and wisdom that our parents wish to share with us. This ongoing dialogue can help us heal, providing clarity as we move forward in our lives while honoring the legacy of love that they left behind.

Ultimately, the nature of spiritual connections offers a pathway to understanding that love is eternal. While the physical absence of a parent can leave a void, the spiritual bond remains unbroken, providing comfort and strength in times of grief. By embracing this reality, we can transform our sorrow into a celebration of the love that continues to flourish beyond the physical realm. In the journey of healing, it is essential to remember that we are never truly alone; our parents are always with us, guiding us with their love from beyond.

Chapter 2:

Grieving the Physical Loss

NAVIGATING THE WAVES OF GRIEF

Grief is a complex journey, one that often feels overwhelming and isolating. When we lose a parent, the emotional waves can crash over us unexpectedly, leaving us vulnerable and struggling to find our footing. It's essential to acknowledge that these feelings are a natural response to loss. Each wave of grief can bring different emotions—sadness, anger, confusion, and even moments of joy as we reflect on cherished memories. Embracing these emotions allows us to process our grief and to understand that it is a testament to the love that we shared with our parents.

As we navigate through this challenging time, it is helpful to remember that love transcends the physical realm. The bond we share with our parents does not end with their passing; instead, it transforms into a deeper spiritual connection. This love can serve as a guiding light, illuminating our path through the darkness of grief. Many individuals find comfort in the belief that their loved ones are still present in spirit, offering support and encouragement as we learn to live without their physical presence. By nurturing this connection, we can draw strength from our memories and the love that never fades.

Finding ways to honor the memory of our parents can also play a significant role in our healing process. This could include creating a memorial, participating in activities they enjoyed, or sharing stories with friends and family that celebrate their lives. Engaging in these practices helps to keep their spirit alive within us and allows our love to flourish even in their absence. By actively remembering and celebrating our parents, we create a space where their influence and teachings continue to guide us, providing a sense of comfort and belonging.

It is crucial to give ourselves permission to grieve and to seek support when needed. Surrounding ourselves with understanding friends, family, or support groups can foster a sense of community during this difficult time. Sharing our feelings and experiences with others who have faced similar losses can create connections that validate our emotions. We are not alone in our journey; many have walked this path and can offer insights and encouragement, reminding us that healing is possible and that love can endure beyond death.

Ultimately, navigating the waves of grief is a personal and unique experience for each individual. While the journey may be challenging, it is also an opportunity for growth and reflection. Embracing the spiritual connection we have with our parents can help us find peace and solace in our memories. As we learn to carry their love within us, we can honor their legacy and continue to live fully, knowing that true love never dies and that our parents will always hold a special place in our hearts.

HONORING THEIR MEMORY

Honoring the memory of our parents is a profound way to celebrate their lives and the love they shared with us. When we experience the loss of a parent, it can feel as though a part of our own identity has been taken away. Yet, in this time of grief, we have the opportunity to preserve their legacy and keep their spirit alive in our hearts. By reflecting on the beautiful moments we shared and the lessons they imparted, we can create a living tribute that transcends the boundaries of life and death. Each memory becomes a thread that weaves the fabric of our ongoing relationship, reminding us that true love never dies.

To honor our parents, we can start by creating rituals that celebrate their lives and the impact they had on us. This could be as simple as lighting a candle in their memory or creating a dedicated space in our home filled with photographs, mementos, and cherished possessions. These physical reminders serve as portals to our past, allowing us to connect with their essence and find comfort in their presence. Celebrating their birthdays or anniversaries through small acts of kindness or community service can also be a beautiful way to channel our love for them, spreading joy in the world just as they did when they were with us.

Sharing stories about our parents with family and friends can further honor their memory. Gathering loved ones to reminisce about the moments that made us laugh, cry, and grow can create a sense of unity and healing. These conversations not only keep their memory alive but also reinforce the bonds between those who knew and loved them. By passing down their wisdom and values, we ensure that their spirit continues to influence our lives and the lives of future generations. In this way, our parents become timeless figures within our family narratives, their love echoing through the years.

Engaging in activities that our parents enjoyed can also serve as a powerful tribute. Whether it is gardening, cooking their favorite recipes, or participating in hobbies they loved, these actions allow us to feel their presence in a tangible way. Each moment spent honoring their passions can evoke feelings of connection and joy, transforming our grief into a celebration of life. As we immerse ourselves in these activities, we may even sense their guidance, offering us comfort and encouragement as we navigate our own paths.

Ultimately, honoring our parents is about recognizing that love transcends the physical realm. While their bodies may no longer be with us, their spirits remain intertwined with ours. By embracing this spiritual connection, we cultivate a deeper understanding of the enduring bond we share. Each act of remembrance, each shared story, and each moment spent in their honor reinforces the truth that love never fades. In this journey of honoring their memory, we find solace, strength, and an unwavering reminder that our parents will always be a part of us, guiding us from beyond.

Chapter 3:

Signs From Beyond

RECOGNIZING SUBTLE MESSAGES

Recognizing subtle messages from loved ones who have passed can be a profound experience, particularly for those navigating the loss of a parent. These messages often come in gentle, unexpected forms, and with an open heart and mind, you can learn to recognize them. Signs may appear in your dreams, through the actions of nature, or even in the thoughts that drift into your mind during quiet moments. Embracing these experiences allows you to feel a continued connection with your parent, reinforcing the belief that love truly transcends physical boundaries.

One of the most common ways in which your parent may communicate is through dreams. Dreams can serve as a bridge between the physical and spiritual realms, allowing for meaningful encounters. When you dream of your parent, pay attention to the emotions you feel upon waking. A sense of comfort, love, or guidance may indicate their presence and desire to reach out. Keeping a dream journal can help capture these moments, making it easier to reflect on their significance and the messages they convey.

Nature often acts as a messenger, too. You might notice a sudden appearance of a butterfly, a cardinal, or even a gentle breeze that seems to carry whispers of love. These signs can feel serendipitous, and it's essential to remain open to their meaning. When you experience these moments, take a moment to breathe deeply and acknowledge the connection you share. Nature has a way of reminding us of the beauty of life and the enduring presence of those we cherish, even after they have departed from this world.

Another way to recognize subtle messages is through the thoughts and feelings that arise unexpectedly. You may find yourself recalling a cherished memory, feeling a sudden rush of warmth, or hearing your parent's voice in your mind. These instances can be seen as affirmations of their ongoing love and support. It's vital to trust these moments and allow them to guide you on your journey of healing. Your parent's spirit may be encouraging you to find joy or pursue your passions, reminding you that their love remains a vital part of your existence.

As you navigate your grief, remember that recognizing these subtle messages can be a source of comfort and hope. They serve as a reminder that true love never dies and that your connection to your parent continues to thrive, even beyond the physical realm. By remaining receptive to these signs, you foster a bond that transcends time and space, allowing their love to guide and inspire you as you move forward in life. Embrace these messages, as they are a testament to the enduring nature of love and the connection that will forever remain in your heart.

DREAMS AS PORTALS OF CONNECTION

Dreams often serve as powerful conduits, allowing us to connect with loved ones who have passed away. For those who have experienced the loss of a parent, dreams can become a sacred space where memories and emotions intertwine. In these ethereal realms, the boundaries of life and death blur, enabling us to experience moments of profound connection. When we close our eyes at night, we open ourselves to the possibility of reuniting with our parents, receiving messages of love, support, and comfort that remind us they are never truly gone.

Many individuals report vivid dreams where they can see, hear, and even embrace their deceased loved ones. These encounters can be so realistic that, upon waking, the emotions linger, leaving us with a sense of peace. Such dreams are more than mere figments of our imagination; they can be interpreted as visits from our parents, reassuring us that their love transcends the physical boundaries of life. Each dream offers a glimpse into the enduring bond we share, allowing us to feel their presence in a tangible way.

In these dreams, parents often convey messages that address our current struggles or fears. They may offer guidance or encouragement, reminding us that they are watching over us and cheering us on from the spiritual realm. This connection can be incredibly healing, as it reassures us that we are not alone in our journey. The wisdom shared in these nighttime encounters serves as a reminder that love is a powerful force that continues to thrive, even when our physical bodies have parted ways.

Moreover, the dreams we experience can act as a catalyst for our own healing process. They provide a unique opportunity to confront unresolved feelings of grief or guilt. By engaging with the emotions that surface during these dreams, we can begin to work through our pain and find solace in the knowledge that our parents want us to be happy. The messages conveyed in these moments can inspire us to cherish our memories and carry the love we shared into our daily lives, fostering a sense of connection that endures beyond the grave.

Ultimately, the dreams we have of our parents serve as a beautiful testament to the idea that true love never dies. They remind us that while our loved ones may no longer be physically present, their spirits continue to exist around us. Embracing these experiences can help us navigate the complexities of grief and loss, allowing us to feel a sense of peace and fulfillment. In the realm of dreams, we discover that the love we shared remains a vibrant part of our existence, bridging the gap between the physical and spiritual worlds, and affirming that we will always hold a special place in each other's hearts.

Chapter 4:

The Language of Love

COMMUNICATING WITH THE DEPARTED

Communicating with the departed can be an empowering journey for those mourning the loss of a parent. While the physical absence can feel overwhelming, the essence of love remains unbroken. Many individuals find comfort in the belief that their loved ones continue to exist in a different form, providing opportunities for connection that transcend the physical realm. By opening ourselves up to signs and messages from beyond, we cultivate a sense of presence that can foster healing and hope.

One of the most profound ways to connect with departed loved ones is through the practice of mindfulness and meditation. These practices create a serene space where one can reflect, remember, and invite messages from their loved ones. During these moments of quiet contemplation, many report feeling a warmth, experiencing vivid memories, or even receiving intuitive insights. This connection often serves as a reminder that love does not die; it evolves into a different, yet equally powerful, form of communication.

Furthermore, many people find solace in the natural world, where signs from their departed loved ones frequently appear. Whether it's a sudden breeze, the flutter of a butterfly, or an unexpected song playing on the radio, these occurrences can feel like a gentle nudge from the other side. By remaining open to these signs, individuals can foster a sense of closeness with their parents, understanding that their love can still be felt in everyday moments. This awareness encourages a dialogue that continues even after physical separation.

Writing can also be a powerful tool for connecting with departed parents. Journaling letters to them allows grieving individuals to express their feelings, share their lives, and ask questions that linger in their hearts. This act of writing not only serves as a form of emotional release but also creates an avenue for receiving guidance and comfort. Many report feelings of clarity and connection, as if their parents are responding through their own thoughts and feelings, reinforcing the idea that love continues to thrive beyond physical barriers.

Embracing the belief that communication with the departed is possible can transform the grieving process into one of celebration and remembrance.

Rather than solely focusing on the absence, individuals can honor the enduring bond they share with their parents. By nurturing this spiritual connection, they can find strength in the knowledge that true love never dies and that their parents are forever a part of their journey, watching over them with unwavering love.

THE POWER OF INTUITION

Intuition is often described as a gut feeling or an instinctive understanding that transcends rational thought. For those who have experienced the loss of a parent, tapping into this innate ability can provide comfort and guidance during a time of profound grief. It serves as a bridge to the spiritual realm, allowing us to connect with our loved ones in ways that words cannot express. By embracing your intuition, you can open your heart and mind to the subtle messages that may come from beyond, reinforcing the idea that true love never dies.

Many people report experiencing signs from their departed loved ones, often described as intuitive nudges or feelings of presence. These signs may manifest as a sudden memory, an unmistakable scent, or even a dream that feels vividly real. Trusting these experiences is crucial, as they can offer solace and reassurance that your parent is still with you in spirit. By acknowledging and embracing these moments, you affirm the bond that remains, reminding yourself that love is an energy that transcends physical boundaries.

Intuition also plays a vital role in self-care during grief. As you navigate the complex emotions that accompany loss, listening to your inner voice can guide you toward healing practices that resonate with your soul. Whether it's seeking solace in nature, journaling your feelings, or engaging in meditation, tuning into your intuition can help you identify what you truly need in your journey. This self-awareness fosters resilience and empowers you to honor your parent's memory while nurturing your own well-being.

Moreover, your intuition can enhance your spiritual connections, helping you to cultivate a deeper understanding of life after loss. Engaging in practices such as mindfulness or energy healing can strengthen your ability to receive messages from the universe. These practices create a safe space for your heart to remain open, allowing for the flow of love and guidance from your parent. Recognizing that your connection with them continues can be a profound source of comfort, reminding you that love is eternal and ever-present.

Ultimately, the power of intuition serves as a beacon of hope and healing in the face of loss. By learning to trust and nurture this inner voice, you can forge a path toward emotional and spiritual growth. The journey through grief may be challenging, but embracing your intuition allows you to feel the presence of your parent, fostering a sense of peace and connection that transcends time and space.

Remember, true love never fades; it evolves, guiding you through the darkness and illuminating the way forward.

Chapter 5:

Healing Through Remembrance

CREATING RITUALS OF LOVE

Creating rituals of love can be a profound way to honor the memory of parents who have passed away, allowing their essence to remain a comforting presence in our lives. These rituals serve as a bridge connecting the physical world with the spiritual, helping us to manifest our love in tangible ways. By establishing practices that resonate with our hearts, we can cultivate a sense of closeness that transcends the boundaries of life and death. Whether it's lighting a candle, planting a tree, or sharing a meal, these acts of remembrance can bring solace and connection to our journey of grief.

One powerful ritual is the creation of a memory box. This box can be filled with mementos that remind us of our parents: photographs, letters, or small items that evoke cherished memories. As we gather these tokens, we are engaging in a sacred act of love, reflecting on the moments that shaped our lives. Each item serves as a reminder of their influence and the bond that remains unbroken. Taking time to revisit this box can provide comfort during difficult days, allowing us to feel their presence and reconnect with the love that remains.

Another beautiful way to honor our parents is through the practice of sharing stories. Gathering family and friends to recount memories can create a warm atmosphere filled with laughter and love. These storytelling sessions not only keep the memory of our loved ones alive but also strengthen the ties between those who share in the experience. By celebrating their lives and the lessons they imparted, we create a living tribute that enhances our connection to them, fostering a sense of community while reinforcing the idea that true love never fades away.

Incorporating nature into our rituals can also be a deeply spiritual experience. Setting aside a special place in a garden or a local park where we can reflect and feel our parents' presence can be incredibly healing. Planting flowers or trees in their memory serves as a reminder of their enduring spirit and a symbol of love that continues to grow. Nature has a unique ability to help us feel grounded and connected, offering a serene space to meditate and nurture our spiritual connections with those we have lost.

Ultimately, creating rituals of love allows us to express our feelings and cultivate a relationship that evolves with time. These practices can be personalized to reflect the unique bond we shared with our parents, ensuring that their love remains a guiding light in our lives. Embracing these rituals not only honors their memory but also fosters healing and hope, reminding us that while their physical presence may be gone, their spirit and love continue to thrive within us. In this journey, we discover that love truly knows no boundaries, allowing us to feel supported and connected to those we hold dear, even from beyond.

CELEBRATING THEIR LEGACY

Celebrating the legacy of our parents is a powerful way to honor their memory and keep their spirit alive in our hearts. When we experience the loss of a parent, it can feel as though a vital part of ourselves has been taken away. However, by focusing on the beautiful moments we shared and the lessons they imparted, we can transform our grief into a celebration of their life. Each cherished memory acts as a thread that weaves their presence into the fabric of our daily existence, reminding us that their love remains a guiding light, even in their absence.

As we navigate through our grief, we may find solace in the rituals and traditions that our parents cherished. Whether it is cooking their favorite meal, listening to their favorite songs, or simply sharing stories with family and friends, these acts become a tribute to their legacy. They create an opportunity for us to connect not only with our parents but also with each other. In sharing these moments, we foster a sense of community and support, allowing ourselves to grieve collectively while celebrating the joy our parents brought into our lives.

In addition to these shared experiences, we can also honor our parents by embodying the values they instilled in us. Reflecting on their teachings and the way they lived their lives can inspire us to carry forward their legacy. Whether it was their kindness, resilience, or sense of humor, we can choose to integrate these qualities into our own lives. By doing so, we not only keep their memory alive but also allow their influence to shape our journey, reminding us that true love transcends the boundaries of life and death.

Finding ways to express our love for our parents can also be a beautiful means of celebration. Writing letters, creating scrapbooks, or engaging in artistic endeavors can serve as powerful outlets for our emotions. These creative expressions become acts of love, allowing us to articulate our feelings and share our journey with them. Even in the silence of their absence, we can communicate with them in our own unique ways, reinforcing the idea that our bond remains unbroken and their presence can still be felt in our lives.

Ultimately, celebrating the legacy of our parents is about recognizing that while they may no longer be physically present, their love continues to resonate within us. We carry their stories, teachings, and memories forward, ensuring that they live on in our hearts and actions. In embracing this celebration, we acknowledge that true love never dies; it transforms, evolves, and connects us to a realm beyond the physical. By honoring our parents in meaningful ways, we not only find healing but also celebrate the enduring power of love that transcends all boundaries.

Chapter 6:

Embracing Spiritual Practices

MEDITATION FOR CONNECTION

Meditation is a powerful tool that can help us reconnect with our loved ones who have passed away, especially our parents. When we experience the profound loss of a parent, it can feel as though a part of us has been severed. However, through meditation, we can cultivate a deeper connection that transcends the physical realm. This practice allows us to quiet the mind, open our hearts, and invite the presence of our loved ones into our lives once more. By embracing meditation, we create a sacred space where love can flourish, reminding us that true love never dies.

As we sit in stillness, we can visualize our parents enveloping us in their warmth and guidance. This visualization can be a source of comfort, helping us to feel their presence surrounding us. Focusing on our breath and letting go of the chaos of our thoughts enables us to connect with the essence of our parents. Each inhale can be a reminder of their love, while each exhale can release the pain of their absence. This cyclic process serves as a bridge between our world and theirs, allowing us to cherish the memories we hold dear and to feel their spirit alive within us.

In these moments of meditation, we may find ourselves receiving messages from beyond. Often, these messages manifest as feelings, sensations, or even thoughts that seem to come from outside ourselves. Our intuition can guide us to understand these communications, helping us realize that our parents are still watching over us, guiding our paths and offering their unwavering support. This connection can be incredibly healing, allowing us to feel less alone in our grief and more attuned to the love that still exists between us.

Practicing meditation regularly can help us maintain this connection over time. By setting aside just a few minutes each day to engage in this practice, we create a ritual that honors our parents' memory. This dedication to meditation fosters a sense of peace and acceptance, allowing us to navigate our grief with grace. As we become more attuned to the spiritual realm, we may notice signs and synchronicities that affirm our connection, reinforcing the idea that our loved ones are never truly gone.

Ultimately, meditation for connection is not just about seeking comfort; it is about celebrating the enduring bond we share with our parents. This practice empowers us to transform our grief into a profound appreciation for the love that remains. By tapping into this divine connection, we honor their legacy and embrace the belief that love transcends the physical realm. In our hearts, we carry their spirit with us, reminding us that even in their absence, our parents continue to inspire, guide, and love us unconditionally.

WRITING LETTERS TO THE DEPARTED

Writing letters to the departed can be a profound and healing experience for those who have lost their parents. It offers a unique opportunity to express feelings that may remain unspoken, to share memories, and to seek comfort in the connection that transcends the physical realm. These letters become a bridge between the living and the departed, allowing for an exchange of love that remains ever-present, even in the face of loss. Embracing this practice can foster a sense of closeness and keep the spirit of your loved ones alive in your heart.

When you sit down to write, let your emotions flow freely. Start by addressing your parent directly, as if they were sitting right next to you. You might begin with a fond memory, recounting a shared experience that brings a smile to your face. This act of remembrance not only honors their legacy but also reinforces the bond you shared. As you write, don't hesitate to express your feelings of sorrow, gratitude, and even joy. Each word serves as a testament to the love that continues to exist, reminding you that true love never dies.

In your letters, feel free to ask questions that linger in your heart. You may wonder about their thoughts on your current life or seek guidance on a decision you must make. Writing these questions down can be a way to invite their spirit into your reflection, creating a dialogue that transcends the boundaries of this world. While you may not receive answers in the traditional sense, many find that insights or comfort come in unexpected ways, affirming the spiritual connection that remains strong even after their physical presence has faded.

In addition to personal reflections, consider expressing your hopes and dreams in these letters. Share your aspirations and the ways you are honoring their memory in your life. This can be a source of strength and motivation, as you recognize that your journey is intertwined with theirs.

Acknowledging their influence in your achievements not only keeps their spirit alive but also reinforces the idea that love and support transcend the physical realm. Your letters become a record of your growth, carrying their essence with you as you navigate life's challenges.

Lastly, make this practice a ritual if it brings you comfort. Whether it's a weekly or monthly tradition, creating a space for these letters can offer solace in moments of grief. You might choose to read them aloud, light a candle, or even create a special place to keep them. Each time you write, you reaffirm the understanding that love is eternal, and that the bond with your parents remains unbroken. Through this heartfelt expression, you honor their memory and cultivate a spiritual connection that will accompany you on your journey, reminding you that you are never truly alone.

Chapter 7:

Shared Experiences Beyond the Veil

STORIES OF CONNECTION

In the quiet moments of grief, when the weight of loss feels most pronounced, many individuals find themselves yearning for signs that their loved ones are still with them. These stories of connection serve as poignant reminders that love transcends the physical realm. The bond you shared with your parent cannot be severed by death; instead, it transforms, allowing for a new kind of communication that can be both comforting and enlightening. Each story illustrates how the essence of love can manifest in unexpected ways, offering solace and a sense of ongoing presence.

Consider the tale of a young woman who, after her mother's passing, felt drawn to her childhood home. One evening, as she flipped through an old photo album, she stumbled upon a picture of her mother holding a butterfly. Suddenly, a butterfly appeared at her window, lingering just long enough for her to feel an unmistakable warmth envelop her. In that moment, she understood that her mother was reaching out, reminding her that their love was still alive and vibrant. Such encounters reinforce the idea that our loved ones often communicate through nature, signs, and symbols that resonate deeply with our hearts.

Another moving account comes from a man who frequently dreamed of his father after his death. In these dreams, they shared conversations that felt incredibly real, filled with wisdom and love. One night, his father reassured him about the decisions he was making in life, guiding him toward a path of fulfillment. Upon awakening, the man felt a renewed sense of purpose and connection. Dreams can serve as a powerful channel for communication, offering comfort and guidance when we need it most. They remind us that even in the dream world, love knows no boundaries.

Many individuals report experiencing a sensation of being watched or guided by their parents in times of need. A grieving daughter shared her experience of feeling an overwhelming sense of calm during a particularly challenging moment in her life. She recalled a time when she was struggling with a major decision, and out of nowhere, she felt her mother's presence, as if she were whispering words of encouragement in her ear. This sensation provided her with the courage she needed to move forward, illustrating how love can manifest in moments of vulnerability. Such experiences are not merely coincidences; they are expressions of love that continue to nurture us from beyond.

As we share these stories of connection, it's essential to remember that our relationship with our parents evolves but never diminishes. The love you shared is eternal, and the bond remains unbroken. Embracing the signs and experiences that come your way can open your heart to the possibility of ongoing connection. Whether through dreams, nature, or moments of inspiration, you can find comfort in knowing that your parent's love is a guiding light, always present and forever illuminating your path.

FINDING COMFORT IN COMMUNITY

In the journey of grief, the importance of community cannot be overstated. When we lose a parent, the emotional landscape can feel incredibly isolating, as if no one else can truly understand the depth of our sorrow. Yet, it is within the embrace of community that we often find solace and strength. Surrounding ourselves with those who share similar experiences allows us to express our feelings without judgment, fostering an environment where healing can begin.

This sense of belonging reminds us that we are not alone in our pain and that others are walking a similar path, each step bringing us closer to acceptance and peace.

True love never fades, and the connections we forge with others during our time of grief can mirror the bond we shared with our parents. In these moments, we discover that love transcends even the deepest loss. Gathering with friends and family who have also experienced the loss of a parent creates a space of understanding where stories are shared, memories are cherished, and emotions are validated. These gatherings become sacred, allowing us to celebrate the lives of our loved ones while simultaneously nurturing our own spirits. In community, we recognize that our parents' love continues to resonate within us, encouraging us to seek joy and connection.

Spiritual connections can deepen our sense of community, intertwining our grief with something greater than ourselves. Engaging in collective rituals, such as lighting candles or sharing messages and memories, provides a profound sense of connection to those we have lost. These shared experiences not only honor our parents' legacy but also allow us to feel their presence in our lives. When we come together in spirit and intention, we create a tapestry of love that reinforces the belief that our parents are still with us, guiding us from beyond the physical realm.

As we navigate the complexities of grief, community offers us tools for healing. Support groups, online forums, and even local gatherings can provide the emotional support we need. Sharing our stories and listening to others can be incredibly cathartic, reminding us that healing is not a solitary journey. The lessons we learn from those around us can help us grow and adapt, transforming our pain into purpose. In these spaces, we find encouragement to honor our parents in ways that feel authentic, creating new traditions and continuing their legacies.

Ultimately, finding comfort in community is about weaving a support network that cultivates love and understanding. It encourages us to speak openly about our feelings and to lean on others when we feel overwhelmed. As we unite with those who understand our journey, we begin to forge new paths of connection. In this shared experience, we realize that while our parents may have transitioned to another realm, their love and influence remain alive within us and among us. Together, we can navigate the tumultuous waters of grief, transforming our sorrow into a source of strength and resilience, fortified by the bonds we share with one another.

Chapter 8:

The Cycle of Life and Love

UNDERSTANDING LIFE AFTER DEATH

Understanding life after death is a profound journey that many embark upon after experiencing the loss of a parent. It challenges the mind and comforts the heart, inviting us to explore the depths of our beliefs about existence beyond the physical realm. The love shared with a parent transcends time and space, suggesting that even in their absence, a connection remains unbroken. This chapter serves as a beacon of hope for those navigating the turbulent waters of grief, offering insights into the nature of love that endures beyond mortality.

The essence of life after death is often perceived through the lens of spiritual connections. Many who have lost loved ones report feelings of their presence, experiencing signs that suggest their continued existence in a different form. Whether it's a gentle breeze, a familiar scent, or a sudden memory that floods the mind, these moments can reaffirm that love is not bound by physical limitations. They serve as reminders that our parents may continue to watch over us, guiding us in ways that transcend our understanding, reinforcing the idea that true love never dies.

Exploring the spiritual realm can bring comfort to those grieving. Engaging in practices such as meditation, prayer, or simply reflecting on cherished memories can create a space for connection with our departed loved ones. These rituals help us acknowledge that although they are no longer with us in body, their energy and essence remain intertwined with ours. This connection fosters a sense of peace, allowing us to feel their love enveloping us in moments of sorrow and solitude.

Furthermore, the concept of life after death encourages us to embrace the legacy our parents leave behind. The values they instilled, the lessons they taught, and the love they shared are all gifts that continue to shape our lives. By honoring their memory and embodying their teachings, we keep their spirit alive within us. This act of remembrance transforms our grief into a celebration of their life, reinforcing that while they may be gone from our sight, they are never absent from our hearts.

Ultimately, understanding life after death invites us to redefine our relationship with grief. It encourages us to see it as a journey rather than a destination, filled with opportunities for growth and connection. The love we experienced with our parents does not fade; it evolves into something more profound. As we navigate our paths forward, we can find solace in the belief that the bonds we share are eternal, assuring us that love indeed knows no boundaries, and our parents remain with us in spirit, forever guiding and loving us from beyond the physical realm.

THE CONTINUITY OF LOVE

In the journey of life, the love we share with our parents is one of the most profound connections we experience. Even in moments of loss, this bond remains unbroken, transcending the physical realm. The continuity of love is a powerful reminder that while our parents may no longer be with us in the way we once knew, their love continues to resonate within us, guiding and supporting us through our lives. This love is not confined to memories; it becomes a part of our very essence, shaping who we are and how we navigate the world.

When we think of true love, we often associate it with moments of joy, laughter, and shared experiences. However, true love also encompasses the lessons, values, and wisdom imparted to us by our parents. These elements of their love are woven into the fabric of our being and remain with us, even after they have passed. Reflecting on the teachings and sacrifices of our parents can provide a source of comfort and strength, reminding us that their love is a guiding force that will always be present.

Spiritual connections can be a source of solace for those grieving the loss of a parent. Many individuals report feeling their loved ones' presence in subtle yet profound ways—through signs, dreams, or moments of quiet reflection. These experiences serve as gentle reminders that love transcends the physical boundaries of life and death. Embracing these spiritual connections can help foster a sense of peace, allowing us to feel our parents' love surrounding us, providing encouragement as we navigate the challenges of life without their physical presence.

As we honor our parents' memory, it is essential to recognize that the love we shared is an everlasting legacy. Celebrating their lives through acts of kindness, sharing stories, or engaging in activities they enjoyed helps keep their spirit alive within us. This continuity of love not only serves as a tribute to our parents but also allows us to cultivate our own capacity for love and compassion, enriching our relationships with others. In doing so, we become living embodiments of the love our parents bestowed upon us.

Ultimately, the continuity of love reassures us that our parents are never truly gone. Their love surrounds us, infusing our lives with meaning and purpose. By embracing this profound connection, we can find comfort in the knowledge that love is an eternal force, bridging the gap between the physical and spiritual realms. In this understanding, we can heal, grow, and continue to share the love we received, honoring our parents and keeping their legacy alive in our hearts.

Chapter 9:

Moving Forward with Love

EMBRACING NEW BEGINNINGS

Embracing new beginnings after the loss of a parent can be one of the most challenging yet transformative experiences in life. The initial wave of grief may feel overwhelming, casting a shadow over the potential for renewal and growth. However, it is essential to remember that every ending carries within it the seeds of a new chapter. By allowing ourselves to honor the love we shared, we can also open our hearts to the possibility of new beginnings. This journey does not mean forgetting; rather, it is about carrying forward the essence of our loved ones in a way that enriches our lives.

As we navigate through the pain of loss, it is crucial to seek out the signs and messages from our loved ones. Many find comfort in the belief that love transcends the physical realm. When we embrace the notion that our parents continue to exist in a spiritual dimension, we can feel their presence guiding us toward new opportunities. This connection can manifest in unexpected ways—a gentle breeze, a favorite song, or a sudden memory that sparks joy. These moments serve as reminders that love never truly dies and that our loved ones are always with us, encouraging us to embrace the future.

Creating rituals can be a powerful way to honor our parents while also embracing new beginnings. Whether it's lighting a candle on special occasions, visiting a place that held significance, or engaging in activities that they loved, these acts can foster a sense of continuity. They allow us to celebrate the lives of our parents while also making space for our own journey. Engaging in these rituals can help bridge the gap between the past and the future, reminding us that while we grieve, we can also grow and transform.

As we learn to embrace new beginnings, it is important to cultivate a mindset of hope and possibility. Each day brings with it the chance to discover new passions, forge new relationships, and create new memories. It is perfectly natural to feel hesitant or fearful about stepping forward into the unknown. However, choosing to view this transition as a journey of growth can help lessen that fear. By letting go of what was and welcoming what can be, we honor our parents' legacy by living fully and authentically.

In this transformative process, self-compassion becomes a vital tool. Allow yourself to feel a spectrum of emotions—joy, sadness, excitement, and apprehension. These feelings are all part of the journey of embracing new beginnings. Seek support from friends, family, or support groups that understand your experience. Sharing your story and hearing others can provide solace and perspective. Ultimately, embracing new beginnings is not about replacing the love we lost but rather about recognizing that love is a powerful force that can inspire us to embark on new adventures, even in the face of loss.

CARRYING THEIR LOVE FOREWARD

Carrying their love forward means embracing the profound bonds we shared with our parents and allowing that love to shape our lives. When we lose someone so dear, it can feel as though a part of us has been irrevocably altered. Yet, in the wake of that loss, we discover that love is not confined to the physical presence of those we cherish. Instead, it transforms into a guiding force that inspires us to live more fully, to honor their memory through our actions and choices. This understanding can bring comfort, reminding us that while our parents may no longer walk beside us, their love continues to illuminate our paths.

As we navigate our grief, we can find solace in the idea that love transcends the boundaries of life and death. Every cherished memory, every lesson imparted, and every moment shared becomes a thread in the tapestry of our existence. By recalling the warmth of their hugs, the sound of their laughter, and the wisdom they offered, we can carry their love forward in meaningful ways. This is not about forgetting the pain of loss but rather about transforming that pain into a powerful tribute to their enduring spirit. Each act of kindness we perform in their name can serve as a beacon of their love, allowing it to ripple outward into the world.

Engaging in activities that honor our parents can be incredibly healing. Whether it's cooking their favorite meal, starting a charitable initiative in their name, or simply sharing stories about them with others, these acts keep their spirit alive. We can create rituals that connect us to their memory, such as lighting a candle on special occasions or visiting places that held significance in our relationship. These rituals serve as reminders of the love that continues to surround us, reinforcing the bond that remains unbroken, even in their absence. By doing so, we acknowledge their influence in our lives and invite their spirit to accompany us on our journey.

In addition to honoring their memory through actions, we can also cultivate a spiritual connection that allows us to feel their presence in our daily lives. Many find comfort in meditation, prayer, or quiet reflection, where they can invite their parents' love into their thoughts and hearts. This connection can bring moments of clarity and reassurance, reminding us that love is a powerful force that exists beyond the physical realm. By nurturing this spiritual bond, we can feel their guidance and support in times of need, helping us to navigate the complexities of life without them.

Ultimately, carrying their love forward is about creating a legacy that reflects their values and the love they shared with us. It encourages us to live authentically, to embrace joy, and to express love freely, just as they did. By embodying their spirit in our actions, we not only honor their memory but also allow their love to flourish, inspiring those around us. In this way, we become vessels for their love, ensuring that it never fades but instead grows stronger, weaving through the fabric of our lives and the lives of others.

Chapter 10:

A Parent's Love Never Fades

THE ENDURING LEAGACY OF LOVE

In the tapestry of life, love weaves the strongest threads that bind us together, transcending the boundaries of time and space. When a parent passes away, the heart may feel shattered, but the love shared remains an enduring legacy that continues to shape our existence. This love does not diminish or fade; instead, it transforms, becoming a guiding force that nurtures our spirit and helps us navigate the complexities of life. We may no longer hear their voice or feel their embrace, but the essence of their love lives on in our memories, actions, and the values they instilled in us.

True love knows no boundaries. It exists beyond the physical realm, embodying a connection that cannot be severed by death. Many who have experienced the loss of a parent report feelings of their presence in moments of joy, comfort, or even challenge. This spiritual connection reminds us that love is not confined to our earthly experience. Instead, it expands into a realm where our loved ones continue to watch over us, offering guidance and encouragement. This bond is a testament to the idea that love is a powerful force, capable of linking our souls even when separated by the veil of death.

As we journey through grief, it is essential to recognize that the teachings of our parents continue to resonate within us. Their love has shaped our character, influenced our decisions, and provided us with a moral compass. Embracing this legacy allows us to carry forward their values and traditions, ensuring that their spirit remains alive in our actions. By honoring their memory, we create a bridge between the past and the present, transforming our sorrow into a celebration of their life and the love they shared with us.

Finding solace in the enduring legacy of love can also inspire us to cultivate connections with others. Just as our parents' love has left an indelible mark on our hearts, we have the opportunity to share that love with friends, family, and even strangers. Acts of kindness, compassion, and understanding can echo the teachings of our parents, creating a ripple effect that extends beyond our immediate circle. In this way, their love becomes a catalyst for healing, fostering deeper connections and reminding us that love is a gift meant to be shared and multiplied.

Ultimately, the legacy of love is a source of strength and resilience. It encourages us to face each day with hope, knowing that our parents are with us in spirit, cheering us on from the other side. Their love provides a foundation upon which we can build our lives, guiding us through challenges and reminding us of the beauty that exists in the world. As we embrace this enduring legacy, we honor their memory, keep their spirit alive, and affirm that true love, indeed, never dies.

FINDING PEACE IN THE CONNECTION

In the journey of navigating grief, many find solace in the realization that love transcends physical existence. The bond shared with a parent does not vanish with their passing; instead, it transforms into a deeper connection that can be felt beyond the confines of the physical world. This profound understanding serves as a guiding light, encouraging individuals to seek out the signs and messages that affirm the continued presence of their loved ones. When we open our hearts and minds to these connections, we cultivate an environment where peace can flourish amidst sorrow.

The moments of quiet reflection often reveal the subtle ways in which our parents communicate with us from the beyond. A gentle breeze, a sudden memory, or a favorite song can stir emotions and remind us that our parents are still with us in spirit. These experiences are not mere coincidences; they are invitations to embrace the love that continues to surround us. By acknowledging these signs, we reinforce our bond, allowing us to feel their love and guidance in our everyday lives. This practice nurtures a sense of peace, helping to ease the pain of loss and fostering a lasting connection.

Engaging in rituals or practices that honor the memory of our parents can also provide a pathway to finding peace. Whether it's lighting a candle, creating a memory album, or simply sharing stories with loved ones, these acts serve as a bridge between our worlds. They remind us that while our parents may no longer be physically present, their essence continues to thrive in our memories and in the love we carry forward. Such rituals can be deeply comforting, offering a sense of belonging in our grief and reinforcing the idea that love is eternal.

In moments of despair, it is essential to remember that seeking connection does not mean bypassing the pain of loss. Instead, finding peace in this connection allows us to honor our grief while simultaneously cherishing the relationship that continues to exist. Embracing this duality can be liberating, as it permits us to feel joy in remembering our parents while still acknowledging our sorrow. This balance fosters resilience and helps us navigate the complexities of grief with a sense of hope, knowing that love prevails over loss.

Ultimately, finding peace in the connection with our parents offers a pathway to healing. It invites us to explore the depths of our love and the myriad ways it persists beyond the physical realm. By embracing this spiritual connection, we can cultivate a space within ourselves that honors our parents while allowing their love to guide us forward. Each step taken in this journey is a testament to the enduring nature of love, reminding us that while our parents may have transitioned to another realm, the bond we share remains unbreakable and everlasting.

ABOUT THE AUTHOR

Dr. Daphne Soares is the Founder of Carousel Moms Business and Leadership Coaching, where she empowers individuals to connect with their inner strength, find peace, and achieve their full potential. A highly respected business and leadership coach, counselor, NLP Master Practitioner, and spiritual guide, Dr. Soares has touched countless lives through her unique approach to personal and professional growth.

As a 19x international bestselling author, including one co-authored with the global legend Les Brown,

Dr. Soares has garnered global recognition for her contributions to literature, personal development, and leadership. Her inspiring work has been featured in prestigious global publications such as The NYC Journal, Thrive Global, GLEBM, Yahoo Finance, and many others in multiple languages. Her expertise has also been highlighted on numerous TV channels, including PTV World, and across various platforms, showcasing her profound impact on the lives of those she coaches.

Dr. Soares' achievements have been recognized globally, including prestigious awards such as the First Place Gold Award, and being declared Coach of the Year. She was also awarded the Global Impact Award by Women Changing the World in the UK and has been featured by the NYC Journal. Additionally, Dr. Soares has been honored for her contributions to women's empowerment and personal transformation by leading organizations. Among her many honors, she had the privilege of meeting Sarah Ferguson, Duchess of York, in person in Windsor, UK.

When not coaching or writing, Dr. Soares cherishes time with her family, including her two children and her brother, Ashley Pinto. Her family's love, along with her spiritual journey, continues to fuel her passion for helping others heal, grow, and thrive.

Messages from Beyond: A Parent's Love Never Fades is Dr. Soares' most heartfelt work, offering readers the opportunity to connect with the eternal love of their own parents and loved ones, even after they have passed away. Dr. Soares reflects on the powerful and eternal bond between parents and children. This deeply personal work is a tribute to her beloved parents, E.C. Pinto—an Advocate of the High Court of Baluchistan and Sindh—and Frank Pinto, whose love and influence have shaped her life and work. Through her spiritual connection, Dr.Soares shares messages of hope, peace, and the understanding that a parent's love transcends the physical realm.

PERSONAL NOTES

Made in the USA
Columbia, SC
09 November 2024

45808588R00041